Sarah Ruhl, *The Oldest Boy*

Sarah Ruhl's plays include *In the Next Room, or the vibrator play* (Pulitzer Prize finalist, Tony Award nominee for best new play); *The Clean House* (Pulitzer Prize finalist; the Susan Smith Blackburn Prize); *Passion Play, a cycle* (PEN American award; the Fourth Freedom Forum Playwriting Award from the Kennedy Center); *Dead Man's Cell Phone* (Helen Hayes Award); *Melancholy Play*; *Eurydice*; *Orlando*; *Demeter in the City* (NAACP nomination); *Late: a cowboy song*; *Three Sisters*; and, most recently, *Stage Kiss* and *Dear Elizabeth*. Her plays have been produced on Broadway at the Lyceum by Lincoln Center Theater; off-Broadway at Playwrights Horizons, Second Stage, and Lincoln Center's Mitzi E. Newhouse Theater; and downtown at Clubbed Thumb and Classic Stage Company. Her plays have been produced regionally all over the country, with premiers at Yale Repertory Theatre, the Goodman Theatre, Berkeley Rep, and many others. Her plays have also been produced internationally and have been translated into more than fourteen languages. Originally from Chicago, Ruhl received her M.F.A. from Brown University, where she studied with Paula Vogel. In 2003 she received the Helen Merrill Emerging Playwright Award and the Whiting Writers' Award. A member of 13P and of New Dramatists, she won a MacArthur Fellowship in 2006 and recently received the PEN Center award for a mid-career playwright, the Feminist Press's 40 Under 40 award, and the 2010 Lilly Award. Her book *100 Essays I Don't Have Time to Write* was one of *The New York Times*'s 100 Notable Books of 2014. She is currently on the faculty at Yale School of Drama and lives in Brooklyn with her family. For more about her work, visit www.sarahruhlplaywright.com.

The
Oldest Boy

The
Oldest Boy

A Play
in Three Ceremonies

Sarah Ruhl

Farrar, Straus and Giroux New York

Farrar, Straus and Giroux
18 West 18th Street, New York 10011

Photograph of the author courtesy of the John D.
and Catherine T. MacArthur Foundation

Library of Congress Cataloging-in-Publication Data
Names: Ruhl, Sarah, 1974–
Title: The oldest boy : a play in three ceremonies / Sarah Ruhl.
Description: First edition. | New York : Farrar, Straus and Giroux, 2016.
Identifiers: LCCN 2015023347 | ISBN 9780374535872 (paperback) | ISBN
    9780374714598 (ebook)
Subjects: LCSH: Mothers and sons—Drama. | Reincarnation—Drama.
Classification: LCC PS3618.U48 O43 2016 | DDC 812/.6—dc23
LC record available at http://lccn.loc.gov/201502334

Designed by Abby Kagan

Our books may be purchased in bulk for promotional, educational,
or business use. Please contact your local bookseller or the Macmillan Corporate
and Premium Sales Department at 1-800-221-7945, extension 5442,
or by e-mail at MacmillanSpecialMarkets@macmillan.com.

www.fsgbooks.com
www.twitter.com/fsgbooks • www.facebook.com/fsgbooks

1 3 5 7 9 10 8 6 4 2

For Yangzom,
and for all the mothering that mothers and non-mothers do.

And for my children:
Anna,
William,
and Hope.

The
Oldest Boy

The Oldest Boy was commissioned by and produced by Lincoln Center Theater (André Bishop, producing artistic director; Adam Siegel, managing director; Hattie K. Jutagir, executive director of development and planning). The first performance was on October 9, 2014, at the Mitzi E. Newhouse Theater.

Cast

MOTHER Celia Keenan-Bolger

THE OLDEST BOY Ernest Abuba

FATHER James Yaegashi

A LAMA James Saito

A MONK Jon Norman Schneider

CHORUS Tsering Dorjee Bawa, Takemi Kitamura, Nami Yamamoto

Creative Team

DIRECTOR Rebecca Taichman

SCENIC DESIGNER Mimi Lien

COSTUME DESIGNER Anita Yavich

LIGHTING DESIGNER Japhy Weideman

SOUND DESIGNER Darron L. West

PUPPET DESIGNER/DIRECTOR Matt Acheson

CHOREOGRAPHY Barney O'Hanlon

STAGE MANAGER Charles M. Turner III

The Oldest Boy was subsequently produced by the Marin Theatre Company in Mill Valley, California (Jasson Minadakis, artistic director; Michael Barker, managing director). The first performance was on September 10, 2015.

Cast

MOTHER   Christine Albright
THE OLDEST BOY   Tsering Dorjee Bawa
FATHER   Kurt Uy
A LAMA   Jinn S. Kim
A MONK   Wayne Lee
PUPPETEERS AND DANCERS   Melvign Badiola, Jed Parsario

Creative Team

DIRECTOR   Jessica Thebus
SCENIC DESIGNER   Collette Pollard
COSTUME DESIGNER   Fumiko Bielefeldt
LIGHTING DESIGNER   Jeff Rowlings
SOUND AND COMPOSITIONS   Chris Houston
PUPPET DESIGN AND CONSTRUCTION   Jesse Mooney-Bullock
CHOREOGRAPHY AND CULTURAL CONSULTANT   Tsering Dorjee Bawa

On April 25, 2016, *The Oldest Boy* will be read at more than ten theaters across the country as a fund-raiser to benefit relief efforts in Nepal on the anniversary of the 2015 earthquake. For more information, go to www.tibetfund.org or www.sarahruhl playwright.com.

People (in order of appearance)
MOTHER   (*American, mid-thirties to mid-forties*)
A MONK   (*Tibetan, younger than the lama*)
A LAMA   (*Tibetan, older than the monk*)
THE OLDEST BOY   (*older than the lama, speaks for and moves the puppet, Tibetan*)
FATHER   (*Tibetan, mid-thirties to mid-forties*)

And, if possible, a small chorus of traditional Tibetan dancers, preferably women. It could also be helpful to have live musicians who play traditional Tibetan music.

If Tibetan actors are unavailable to play the Father, Monk, Lama, and The Oldest Boy, I put my trust in the collective imagination and in creative casting.

Puppet
A BOY   (*Two, then three, years old. The puppet has a wonderful face, bright eyes, and big red cheeks.*) In the first production we used a *bunraku* puppet, with the head puppeteer voicing the puppet and the two other puppeteers dancing in the chorus. One could also imagine using a rod puppet or a marionette puppet. We chose a *bunraku* puppet to maximize the expressiveness of the child.

Place
Any North American city with a large Tibetan community, for instance, New York, Boston, Minneapolis, Toronto, Chicago, Berkeley, or Seattle. Then, in Act Two, a monastery in India.

Pronunciation and Definitions

A lama (*pronunciation*, lah-ma): a spiritual teacher, or high-ranking Buddhist monk.

A *tulku* (*pronunciation*, tuhl-koo): a high-ranking lama who can choose his own rebirth.

Rinpoche (*pronunciation*, rhin-poh-chay): a title meaning "precious one"; often, but not always, used to designate *tulku*s, or reincarnated lamas.

Dharamsala (*pronunciation*, Dar-um-sal-a): home of the Dalai Lama in India, and the Central Tibetan Administration.

Some Notes

Tibet has an ancient monastic tradition of finding living reincarnations of their high lamas, including the Dalai Lama. About one-fifth of the population traditionally takes monastic vows. China invaded Tibet in 1949, under the leadership of Mao. More than a million Tibetans died as a direct result of the occupation, 6,256 monasteries were destroyed and looted, and only 14 remain intact. In 1959 the Dalai Lama fled to India, and many Tibetans followed him to Dharamsala, the center of the exiled Tibetan government. The Tibetan people find themselves in exile, spread across India, Nepal, and the Western world, their culture under attack, their people refugees, and their country a victim of ethnic cleansing. Now that Tibetan Buddhism has spread westward, reincarnated lamas are occasionally found outside of Tibet and sometimes, very rarely, are born to non-Tibetans. But the following story is an imagined one. I hope with humility, reader, that you will help me with the bits I got wrong.

If you relate to your teacher as a Buddha, you will receive the blessings of a Buddha. If you relate to your teacher as an ordinary human being, you will get the blessings of an ordinary human being.

—SOGYAL RINPOCHE, *The Tibetan Book of Living and Dying*

Act One

───────

ONE

A tasteful house decorated with rich Tibetan colors.
Half Western furniture, half Eastern furniture and rugs.
A few large statues of the Buddha.

A woman, the mother, sits on the stage.
She places a candle on the floor, faces the audience, and tries to meditate.
She closes her eyes.
She opens her eyes.
She sees the audience.

She stops meditating.
She takes her cushion and candle and turns around and faces the back
*   wall.*
She meditates.
On a baby monitor, a baby cries.
The mother stops meditating.
She goes to the monitor. She listens. The baby stops crying.
She goes and gets a bag of potato chips and starts eating from it.
She pages through a book about child-rearing:
something like Dr. Sears's Attachment Parenting Book.

The doorbell rings.

She jumps. It is unexpected.
She puts down the potato chips.
She goes to the door.
Two Tibetan monks are at the door.
One is a Rinpoche (a high lama or teacher),
the other is a simple monk.

MOTHER
Hello?

LAMA
Hello.

MONK
Hello.

An awkward pause.

MOTHER
Hi.

MONK
Excuse me—sorry to disturb you—you are the babysitter?

MOTHER
The babysitter? No.

LAMA
You are a friend of the house?

MOTHER
Um—this is my house.

MONK
But—you are the mother of the house?

MOTHER
Yes—I am the mother of the house.

MONK
Oh, I see.

LAMA
Perhaps we have the wrong house?

MOTHER
I don't know—sorry—I wasn't expecting you.

LAMA
Nor we you!

They laugh.

MOTHER
Perhaps you are looking for my husband?

LAMA
Your husband owns a restaurant in town?

MOTHER
Oh, yes.

LAMA
Then it is he we have come to visit.

MOTHER
Oh!

MONK
Rinpoche is visiting from India.

MOTHER
Oh, I see! Welcome! Rinpoche.

He bows his head.
She bows awkwardly.

MOTHER
Would you like to come in?

MONK and **LAMA**
Yes, yes, thank you.

LAMA
I have been to your husband's restaurant once, long time ago. Very delicious.

MOTHER
Of course I think so, but I'm biased. Would you like some tea?

MONK   **LAMA**
Oh yes yes, we would love some tea, thank you.   Thank you, yes.

MOTHER
I'm so sorry—if I'd known you were coming, I would have—
cleaned and—cooked—and—

MONK and **LAMA**
No, no.

MOTHER
I can at least make you tea.

She exits to put the teakettle on to boil.
The boy cries a little on the baby monitor.
The monks listen attentively, with joy.

LAMA
A baby!

The mother pokes her head back in.

MOTHER
I'm just going to get my son. Are you all right for a moment?

MONK and **LAMA**
Oh, yes yes.

MOTHER

You must excuse me—my husband won't be back from work for another hour. Would you like to come back then?

LAMA

Oh, that is fine, we can wait. You can bring the baby here, if you like. How old is the baby?

MOTHER

Almost three!

MONK

That's good!

MOTHER

Good? Yes—

LAMA

A nice age, yes?

MOTHER

Yes.

A pause in which the baby is quiet.

MOTHER

It sounds as if he's gone back to sleep.

MONK

Yes, he's sleeping now. We can wait.

MOTHER
For my husband?

LAMA
Yes, thank you for your hospitality.

MOTHER
Please—make yourself at home.

MONK and **LAMA**
Thank you, thank you.

MOTHER
You are from India?

LAMA
Yes Dharamsala.

MOTHER
Oh! How wonderful.

MONK
Yes, it is good to be so close to His Holiness the Dalai Lama.

MOTHER
Yes, of course.
Were you born in Tibet?

LAMA
Yes.

MOTHER
Oh! And you too?

MONK
Not me. I have never seen my country.

MOTHER
Oh, I'm sorry—I mean—

MONK (*making a gesture of "don't be sorry"*)
I was born in Nepal.

MOTHER
My husband lived in Nepal. After leaving Tibet.

MONK
Oh, yes yes.

MOTHER
You know my husband?

LAMA
We know of your husband.

MOTHER
But you haven't met?

LAMA
No.

A pause.

MOTHER
My husband isn't famous. He's a good cook, but he's not famous.
Is he?

MONK
We have heard of his restaurant! I have dreamed of it, in fact.

MOTHER
You have?

They nod.

LAMA
I will tell you a little story.
There was once a man who had four wives.

MOTHER
Are you trying to tell me something?

LAMA
Yes. So. This man has four wives. His first wife loved him very
much, but he paid no attention to her. The second wife was
younger and prettier, and he was always chasing after her, fearful
that she would find another man. He tried to keep her. The third
wife was a very practical woman, always gave the husband good
advice, he relied on her. The fourth wife was the youngest, and oh
how he loved to pamper her (*laughs*) oh like this with the youngest wife (*gestures of pampering*), and he gives her everything she

wants, but she is a silly woman. When the man is on his death-bed, he says, "Okay wives, which of you will come with me to death?"

MOTHER
Oh!

LAMA
He asks his fourth wife, "Will you follow me to death?" She says, "No, I will not, I will go find another man after you die."

The monk laughs.
Then the mother laughs.

LAMA
So he asks the third wife, the practical one, "Will you go with me?" She says, "No. No one can go with you to death."

MOTHER
She has a point.

LAMA
Mmm. So he asks his second wife, the pretty one, "Will you go to death with me?" And she laughs at him and says she is too busy, find someone else. So finally he asks his first wife, who was always loyal to him, and she says, "I will go with you."

MOTHER
Wow, so she killed herself?

LAMA
Not really it is just a story.

MOTHER
Oh.

LAMA
You see, the man is just a man.

MOTHER
Uh-huh.

LAMA
His wives are—fourth wife, his body—third wife, his family—second wife, his possessions—but his first wife—his first wife is what you might call his soul. Only his soul can come with him after death.

MOTHER
Oh I like that! I was worried you were going to tell me my husband has another wife in India!

They laugh.

LAMA
Oh no nothing like that!
It is a story about how your consciousness comes with you when you die, it is the only thing of value, the rest is left behind.

MOTHER
I like that. Thank you.
Oh, your tea, excuse me!

MONK and **LAMA**
Thank you.

They incline their heads politely.
She exits.

LAMA (*to the monk, in Tibetan*)
Khong bhot pa-shig dang changsa gyab yo-rey sam jung?
(But I thought he married a Tibetan woman?)

MONK (*in Tibetan*)
Derang sam jung.
(Yes, I thought so.)

LAMA
I did not expect an American woman.

MONK (*in Tibetan*)
Khang pa norpa ma re pey?
(Could this be the wrong house?)

LAMA (*shrugging, in Tibetan*)
Yin gi ma rey. Yin na-yang ha gogi ma rey.
(I don't think so. Then again, one never knows.)

She returns with the tea, overhearing a little bit of their Tibetan.
She responds in Tibetan.

MOTHER (*in Tibetan*)
Ga re sung pa?
(What did you say?)

LAMA
You speak Tibetan?

MOTHER
A little. I'm trying.
Here's your tea.

(*Then in Tibetan:* the tea)
Sol-ja.

She fumbles with the tea a little.
She tries to be formal with them.
She kneels at their feet and serves them.

LAMA and MONK (*in Tibetan*)
Lags-so.
(Thank you.)

The lama takes a sip.

LAMA
Very good!

MOTHER

I hope it's all right. I'm honored to have you here. Did my husband ask you to come? A blessing? For the house? Or the baby?

LAMA

Very good tea! Just like in Tibet. How did you learn to make real butter tea?

MOTHER

My mother-in-law taught me. She went back to Nepal because she said she wanted to die in a place where the tea tasted familiar. With salt. And butter.

LAMA

Yes, yes.

MONK

Of course.

LAMA

You are Buddhist?

MOTHER

Kind of.

They laugh.

LAMA

Kind of?

MOTHER

I was raised Catholic.

LAMA

So you are Catholic?

MOTHER

I think when you are born Catholic, you are always sort of Catholic—but when I grew up, I didn't believe in some of the—things—and then there were those—sort of—problems?—in the church—you know—and somehow I never believed that only the pope could talk to God—it seemed sort of silly—and the Catholic children I knew weren't very nice and I wasn't sure how Catholicism was contributing to their ethical natures—and then I became an atheist and waved Bertrand Russell's "Why I'm Not a Christian" around for a while—and then my father died and I had a dream, and in the dream these huge letters in silver spelled out "There is no God," written across the heavens, and I turned to my father in the dream, and I said, "But who could have written that in the heavens?" and he said, "Exactly." And since then I have been looking for God—

LAMA

Very interesting. Please go on.

MOTHER

And then I met my husband, and I thought he was a very good person, and he was Buddhist, and I liked that Buddhism was scientific—and rational—

LAMA
You are a scientist?

MOTHER
Oh. No—

LAMA
But you are rational—

MOTHER
Am I rational?—I am, I was—a literature professor—

LAMA (*impressed*)
Oh!

MOTHER
Well, I was ABD—
All but dissertation . . . funny term, long story—I was an adjunct—

MONK
Adjunct?

MOTHER
A very badly paid teacher.
What was I saying?

LAMA
You liked rationality—

MOTHER

Yes, I liked rationality, but I wanted something spiritual—sorry is that a stupid word?

MONK

No no—

MOTHER

—that was also rational, and Buddhism seemed rational—and it made me happy—well happier.

LAMA

You have taken refuge?

MOTHER

Not yet. I'm studying now. I don't know enough.

LAMA

It is good you are studying. Buddhists do not like to convert people—never—and His Holiness the Dalai Lama feels it is better for people to worship the way they were taught as children because it is better if you talk to God in your first language, but if you find peace with Buddhism then that is good.

MOTHER

I hope so.

I try to meditate.

I was—trying to meditate when you arrived.

LAMA
Ah?

MOTHER
But I'm not very good. I get distracted.

LAMA
Yes yes, we all get distracted. Even monks.
The effort is the important thing.
Do you have a meditation teacher?

MOTHER
No—just books.

LAMA
You need a teacher. Books are—books.

MOTHER
Yes.

A baby cry starts then stops on the baby monitor.

MOTHER
Oh, I thought I heard Tenzin.
He usually wakes around now from his nap. I might have to feed
him.

MONK (*surprised*)
You are still breast-feeding?

MOTHER (*embarrassed*)
Just a little bit.

MONK
That's good! That's how we Tibetans do. We breast-feed until at least two years, often longer.

MOTHER
In this country we call it attachment parenting.

MONK
What is that—?

MOTHER
Oh it's—you wear your child around, you breast-feed for a long time, you sleep in the same bed as the child . . .

LAMA
Ah the same in Tibet!

MOTHER
Oh really? Then I must ask you: How do you get the child out of the bed after three years?

LAMA
You send them to boarding school!

He laughs. She laughs.

MOTHER

But really.

LAMA

Really! But why, if you'll excuse me, is all this—the wearing the child, the sleeping with the child—called attachment parenting?

MOTHER

It's just this theory—or fashion—that your baby will be more happy, more secure, if they are more—attached.

LAMA

Ha ha! And yet you practice nonattachment!

MOTHER

Well, yes—but I guess not as a mother.

She laughs.
He looks at her keenly.

LAMA

Do you think attachment is the same as love?

MOTHER

No Yes No. Do you?

LAMA

I can tell you it is not the same. Maybe there is a problem in the translation. Affection between a mother and a child, that is natural, that is good, you don't have to do "attachment parenting" to

28

have love. Attachment is grasping, clinging, it is not comfortable. It seems that American mothers are worried their children will not attach to them?

MOTHER
I guess so.

LAMA
But of course a child will attach to a mother, no? This is natural, am I right?

The baby cries "Mama" on the baby monitor.

MOTHER
Oh! It *was* him. Excuse me.

MONK
Of course.

LAMA
Of course.

They sit silently, praying, holding their prayer beads.
She returns with the boy, who is a puppet.
An old man controls the puppet and speaks for him.

MOTHER
This is Tenzin.

OLDEST BOY
Hello.

MONK
Hello, Tenzin.

OLDEST BOY
Hello.

The monk touches the boy's finger.
The boy reaches out and touches the lama's face with great love.

OLDEST BOY
Lama.

MONK
He knows you!

MOTHER (*not understanding, with humor*)
He appears to, yes.

MONK
He was a good baby, a calm baby?

MOTHER
Preternaturally calm.

LAMA
Ah yes. Good boy.

She gives the boy to the lama, who sits down with him happily.
The monk takes a cell phone out and takes a picture of the lama and
  the baby.

MONK
Is it okay?

MOTHER
Oh, yes, of course.

LAMA
May I ask you, did you have any special dreams when you were
carrying him?

MOTHER
Yes. I dreamed twice that the baby was a dog.

OLDEST BOY
A dog, Mama?

LAMA
A dog? And?

MOTHER
A blue dog. Like Egyptian stone. So in the dream I called him
Mister Cobalt Blue.

LAMA
Mister Cobalt Blue.

MOTHER

Yes.

And I dreamed that the baby came out and talked immediately, and had the face of an old man. It was disconcerting.

LAMA

Ah yes, yes! (*He laughs.*)

MONK

If you will excuse me, what was his birth like? What was the weather like outside?

MOTHER

The weather?

MONK

Yes.

MOTHER

Let's see . . . it was April, but there was a snowstorm. I remember we were worried leaving the hospital because of the roads.

LAMA

Are there frequently snowstorms here in April?

MOTHER

Not really.

OLDEST BOY

Bell!

The baby grabs the monk's bell and plays with it.

MOTHER
No no, honey, don't play with his bell.

OLDEST BOY
Why?

The baby plays with the bell.

MOTHER
I said no.

She takes the bell.

LAMA
Please, you mustn't scold him. It is his bell.

MOTHER
What?

The lama bows to the baby.
The baby pats the lama's head, a kingly gesture.
The mother stares.

The door opens.
It is the father.

MOTHER
Uh—my husband—

She goes to him.

MOTHER
Honey, there are some . . . monks here . . .

The father bows formally to the monks.

OLDEST BOY
Papa!

FATHER (*in Tibetan to the monks*)
Tashi delek. Nye-nang la pheb pa di ngatso sode chenpo rey
samgi dug.
(What an honor, hello, welcome. I am lucky to have your
blessings.)

LAMA and **MONK**
Tashi delek.
(Hello.)

FATHER (*to Tenzin*)
Hello.
(*in Tibetan, to the monks*)
Sol-ja phulga?
(Can I get you tea?)

LAMA (*in Tibetan*)
Lag min kherang gi achala ki kyak song.
(No. No, your wife already served.)

Nge norshag. Kherang gi bopa shik dhang trungsa gyabpa ma rey pai?
(Maybe I made a mistake. Haven't you married a Tibetan woman?)

FATHER
Amala gi bodpa thabshe nang pa rey. Leyla khong rang koe shag.
(My mother tried, but it didn't happen. Karma decided.)

LAMA
La rey! Le la koepa ma tok nang wey gongshog min dug.
(Yes, yes. Whatever karma decides, will be.)

MOTHER
What were you saying?

FATHER
I said my mother tried an arranged marriage, but it didn't work. This is my wife, my—uh—my destiny? And he said something like, what you wish doesn't always come, your destiny comes instead.

MOTHER
Oh.

LAMA (*to mother and father*)
You have a very special child. I have known him for a long time. How long now? Thirty-five years? But before that too! (*The boy laughs.*)
(*to the puppet*): Oh yes, I know your sense of humor.
Excuse my jubilation. Your boy is my teacher. My teacher, who died three years ago.

The mother faints into her husband's arms.

Interlude.
In front of the domestic space,
a chorus might come on and do a traditional Tibetan dance.

TWO

The father picks the mother up.
They go back in time.

MOTHER
We met—

FATHER
How did we meet?

MOTHER
He was supposed to marry another woman.

FATHER
An arranged marriage.

MOTHER
I walked into his restaurant. I was in despair—coming from a funeral in the rain—my teacher had just died—I couldn't write, I couldn't read, I couldn't finish my thesis—

FATHER
A crisis of faith? She was beautiful.

MOTHER

I walked to a part of town I'd never been to before—it was that weird time between lunch and dinner, and nothing was open—and the rain started to pour. I had no umbrella—I was looking for some kind of temporary refuge, I suppose—I saw prayer flags and this bright window—out of nowhere—this little tiny restaurant—

FATHER

I was about to close, but I stayed open for her—

A gate, or door, appears.
It might be an invisible gate.
She walks in, wet from the rain.
She sits down over a steaming bowl.
There is no real food inside.

MOTHER

I ate his food—
Dumplings, *momos*—

FATHER

There was no one else in the restaurant that day—

MOTHER

Oh the food was so good—chutneys, vegetables, hot barley soup—*tsampa*—

FATHER

And we talked, over tea—

MOTHER
Of movies—

FATHER
And tattoos—

MOTHER
How I have a strange dread of them—

FATHER
How my sister got an Om Mani Padme Hum, which is a very
important prayer for us, tattooed on her arm, and she said, very
proud, "Look, Mom, I got an Om Mani Padme Hum tattoo!"
And my mom said, "Oh, now you will wander around hell
forever in the afterlife, because you have a tattoo!"

MOTHER
Really?

FATHER
Yes!

MOTHER
And we talked—

FATHER
And it rained—
How my mother carried me on her back, escaping from Tibet
after the Chinese occupation.

MOTHER

Walking over the mountains at night.

FATHER

How cold my feet were—how one of my toes was frostbitten—

MOTHER

How he warmed them in his mother's dress.

FATHER

How when I was two, Chinese soldiers made me pick flies from the excrement of animals. One by one, all the children had to collect fifteen flies apiece—

MOTHER

Why?

FATHER

To show that everyone, including children, should work. (*pause*) Anyway . . .

MOTHER

How I was born in Cincinnati and had a real American childhood—

FATHER

Aggressively wholesome, I think she said?

MOTHER

Yes.

FATHER

And how she was studying religious devotion in the work of atheist American writers—which I did not really understand—Why is there religious devotion in the books of those who are nonbelievers?

MOTHER

I suppose I separate the author from the book—

FATHER

How can you do this?

MOTHER

Exactly! Maybe you can't—or shouldn't—anyway, it seems pointless now. My teacher just died.

FATHER

I'm sorry.

MOTHER

Thank you. Thank you. Anyway, my teacher was the only one who supported my work—and now they'll most likely replace him with this young Marxist literary critic who drives a Jaguar . . .

FATHER

Do intellectuals in your country still believe in Marxism? Do they not see the pain communism has caused so many people?

MOTHER

For them it's not really about real people's pain. They write books about books.

FATHER

I understand! But not really, I don't understand!

MOTHER

Me neither.

They laugh.

MOTHER

I have always loved books since I was a child—and so I wanted to devote my life to them—but without my teacher—who understood that books could be about virtue—or, or—meaning—I feel like the English department is the worst place in the world for a person who loves books . . . Maybe I'll give up my studies. I could do something else.

FATHER

Oh but you mustn't give up your studies!

MOTHER

Why not?

FATHER

No one can take your education away from you. It is one of the few things people cannot steal.

MOTHER

Where were you educated?

FATHER

I was educated at an English boarding school with the sons of princes in Darjeeling—

MOTHER

Oh!

FATHER

—and here I am, now I own a restaurant.

MOTHER

How did you come to own a restaurant?

FATHER

My father died young. I had to support my family. I was the most gifted with languages, and so I gave up my studies, came home from boarding school, and cooked to earn money for my family. I knew four languages, so I could more easily talk to customers. My youngest brother finished his education.

MOTHER

You were the most gifted in languages so you had to give up your education.

FATHER

Yes. But it's okay, I like to cook.

MOTHER
You're a very good cook. Your food—it's—

FATHER
What—

MOTHER
I don't know how to describe it.
It's—

She searches for the word.

MOTHER
It's—*food.*

FATHER
And then—

Pause. They turn toward each other.

MOTHER
Something is stopping me—

FATHER
What?

MOTHER
Something's stopping me from leaving your restaurant. It's the most beautiful room I've ever been in. Like I want to live here.

FATHER
You want to live in my restaurant?

MOTHER
It's like the food I ate before was cardboard and had no nourishment. I want to eat your food forever.

FATHER
Did you actually say that to me?

MOTHER
No, I thought it, I think.

FATHER (*to the audience*)
The light was changing. Darker. More rain. Harder rain. No other customers.

MOTHER
I guess it's time for me to go.

FATHER
I should close the restaurant.

MOTHER
Should I go?

FATHER
Do you have an umbrella?

MOTHER
I forgot one. I always forget one.

FATHER
Then maybe you should wait out the worst of the rain?

MOTHER
Thank you.
Can I help you clean up?

FATHER
Oh, no. No.

MOTHER
Why not?

FATHER
You're a customer. That's silly. I can clean up.

MOTHER
But I have nothing to do. I didn't even bring a book.
I feel silly drinking tea while you clean up after me.

FATHER
There is not much to do—

MOTHER
I want to help you. I want to do the dishes with you.

FATHER
You do?

MOTHER
Yes.

FATHER
Well, all right. Then I can't charge you for your meal.

MOTHER
Oh, that's all right.

FATHER
I insist.

MOTHER (*as in "now our relations have entirely changed"*)
Then I'm no longer a customer.

FATHER
No.

MOTHER
We put our arms into soapy warm water.

FATHER
We didn't talk.

MOTHER
We washed dish after dish.

FATHER
Well, I washed.

MOTHER
I dried.

FATHER
I like washing.

MOTHER
I like drying.

They wash dishes for a while.
These might be real dishes, or imaginary.
In any case, the audience's attention slows
as they experience the feeling, real or imagined,
of soap and water.

MOTHER
I always thought I hated washing dishes. But it's nice to just dry a dish in the rain.

FATHER
You want to give up being a university professor, and be a dish-washer?

MOTHER
Maybe.

FATHER

I handed her the last wet dish.

MOTHER (*about the dish*)

Oh it's slippery—

He moves to help her so she doesn't drop it.
They look at each other.
They kiss.
She drops the soapy dish.

MOTHER

Oh I'm so sorry. It's such a beautiful dish.

FATHER

No no, that's fine. It's nothing—

MOTHER

I'll buy you a new dish—I insist—

FATHER

No! No no no—no.

MOTHER

What is it?

FATHER

I'm engaged to marry a woman I have never met?

MOTHER
What?

FATHER
From India. A Tibetan woman. My family arranged the marriage.

MOTHER
Oh!

FATHER
Yes. I'm to meet her in two weeks.

MOTHER
Then we have something in common. I'm also engaged.

FATHER
To who?

MOTHER
I forget.

FATHER
You forget.

MOTHER
It's no longer relevant.

FATHER
And so I turned the open sign to closed.
The closed sign now faced the world, the open sign now faced us.

MOTHER
And that was that.

FATHER
There were some difficulties along the way.

Time changes.
The gate disappears.
If the gate was invisible, then the invisible gate disappears.

MOTHER
But why?

FATHER
I have to marry someone of my culture. My culture is dying. It's like salt dissolving into water, my people dissolving. If you put a small amount of salt into a very large pool of water, and take a sip, the water is no longer salty. It disappears.

MOTHER
I will become Tibetan—

FATHER (*overlapping*)
You cannot become Tibetan—

MOTHER (*overlapping*)
Let me finish. Tibetan Buddhist—

FATHER
What do you know about Tibetan Buddhism?

MOTHER
I read a book by the Dalai Lama—

FATHER
A book—

MOTHER
Yes. I liked it—

FATHER
You liked it—okay—

MOTHER
I bought it in the Cincinnati airport—

FATHER
Uh-huh—

MOTHER
It made sense to me—philosophical, not dogmatic—how to be happy—and compassionate—

He groans.

MOTHER
I could—what's that thing you do—when you sort of convert—or get baptized as a Buddhist?

FATHER
Take refuge?

MOTHER

Yes—take refuge!—that's such a nice phrase—did you take refuge?

FATHER

I was born into Buddhism, I didn't have to take refuge—

MOTHER

I could take refuge in you.

FATHER

No! No no no . . .

MOTHER

Oh—I'm sorry—that must have sounded—sacriligious—

FATHER (*overlapping with "sacriligious"*)

Oh my mother . . . my mother would be so sad . . .
And my father—my father would be so mad . . .

MOTHER

But do you love me?

FATHER

Yes, of course.

MOTHER

So?

FATHER

So in my country it is not like: oh I love you so that's the end of that. Love is not just this private romantic paradise. There is duty and family—

MOTHER

But you moved *here*.

FATHER

Yes.

MOTHER

So maybe you moved here for a reason.

FATHER

Yes—to earn a living and to avoid being put in a Chinese labor camp because I own a book by His Holiness the Dalai Lama!

MOTHER

Yes, of course. *Of course.* But I mean—you did move here. And here, if you love someone, then—

FATHER

Then—

MOTHER

Then—you choose them.

He laughs.

FATHER
Americans like to choose things. You choose things all the time. I would like: a soy chai latte, wet, with extra foam. You have these preferences. And you believe that these preferences reflect your identity, and that's all you believe. When it's convenient you are religious. When it's not convenient you are not religious. When it's convenient you help your family. When it's not convenient you do not help your family. When your mother is able-bodied, you have her babysit your children. When your mother is old, you put her in a home. It's not like that in my country.

MOTHER
I wish you wouldn't say "you"—like I'm like all Americans.

FATHER
You're right. I'm sorry.
Look, the woman—is flying in to meet me next week.
My family knows her family. She's from a good Tibetan family. It is already arranged. They consulted an astrologist. They know from our birth signs that we are compatible.

MOTHER
Do you believe in all that?

FATHER
Not the astrology part maybe.

MOTHER
What if you hate her?

FATHER
I won't hate her. My family knows her family.

MOTHER
What if she's horrible?

FATHER
She won't be horrible.

MOTHER
What if you don't love her?

FATHER
Then I will come to love her.

MOTHER
Did your parents love each other?

FATHER
Yes.
Kind of.
Did your parents love each other?

MOTHER
Yes. Kind of.

FATHER
It is the same—see, chosen or unchosen.
What about the man you are to marry?
Have you told him?

MOTHER
Yes.

FATHER
What did he say?

MOTHER
It doesn't matter.
I love you.
I choose you.

FATHER
I think you just like my food.

MOTHER
I don't like your food. I love your food.

FATHER
Thank you.

MOTHER
So?

Pause.

FATHER
I'm sorry. I cannot disappoint my family. My family is everything
for me.

MOTHER
Yes.
I understand.
Thank you for this—time we had. I won't forget you.
I think you are good.
And I loved your food. And your ankles. I'm being stupid.
Sorry. Goodbye.

She cries and starts to flee.

FATHER
Wait! Don't go. I can't stand you being sad.

He kneels at her feet.

FATHER
Don't be sad.
Please.

MOTHER
I can't help it.

FATHER
Your sadness . . .
It will break me.

MOTHER

I'm sorry.

FATHER

You are breaking me like in half.

MOTHER

I'm sorry.

FATHER

You are breaking my family . . .

MOTHER

I don't want to break your family. I'm just sad, that's all.

FATHER

Marry me.

MOTHER

Yes, please.

They kiss.

Ceremony One

They get married.
A traditional ceremony.
The mother might wear a traditional chuba—
a colorful apron that Tibetan women wear when they get married.
A procession.
A white horse. Or an approximation thereof.
White scarves.
Throwing barley into the sky.
The ceremony suddenly stops.

FATHER
That is how our wedding would have been in Tibet.

Then, the sound of traffic.
And modern confusion.
And modern costume.
And the silence of bureaucracy.

MOTHER
But we couldn't go to Tibet.

FATHER
We went to city hall, in the morning, before the restaurant opened.

MOTHER
We went alone.

FATHER

I didn't tell my family we were going. They were very angry with me.

MOTHER

I was pregnant. Just a little bit pregnant.

FATHER

A stranger served as our witness and took our picture with an iPhone.

MOTHER

We looked very happy.

FATHER

I sent the picture to my mother in Nepal.
My mother didn't like her.

MOTHER

Actually, I think your mother hated me.

FATHER

My mother doesn't hate anyone. My mother is a very devout woman.

MOTHER

Well, insofar as it was permissible within her religion, she hated me.
And then I had the baby.

FATHER

And oh how my mother loved this baby.

MOTHER

And so she loved me.

It's funny how a child can be an olive branch.

FATHER

She always wanted a grandson.

MOTHER

She came over to meet the baby. She and I stayed up long into the night together, passing the baby back and forth. We were very close.

FATHER

Then she went back to Nepal. She didn't mention I'd married an American woman. I don't think she lied; she just didn't mention that I'd called off the arranged marriage. Instead, she told everyone about the baby. It was her dying wish, she said, to meet the baby.

MOTHER

And then she died. In her country, where the tea tasted the way tea is supposed to taste. With salt and butter. And he could not get to her funeral in time. Because he's a man without a passport.

Instead, every day we filled seven bowls with water.

FATHER

We lit butter lamps. We said prayers for her to have a good re-birth.

Ceremony Two

They fill seven bowls with water.
They say a prayer in Tibetan.
They light incense and butter lamps.

The mother falls over.

THREE

Going back to the end of the first scene.
The father picks up the mother from a faint.
The monk hovers over her, fanning her.
The baby cries.

OLDEST BOY
Mama!

MONK
Should I get her water?

The mother comes out of her faint.

MOTHER (*to her husband*)
Ah! Oh good, I'm here. I had a bad dream that your mother died and someone was taking Tenzin away.

She sees the monk.

MOTHER (*remembering all that's happened*)
Oh! Hello.

FATHER
Rinpoche. Might we have a moment?

LAMA
Yes, of course. I am very sorry we have disturbed her. Perhaps we can call on you later?
We are staying at the Holiday Inn. If you want to reach us.

FATHER
Thank you.

LAMA
If we can arrange a time on this visit to do a formal examination of the child, that would be best. But I think she needs some time.

FATHER (*in Tibetan*)
Lags-so. Thugs je che, Rinpoche.
(Yes. Thank you very much, Rinpoche.)

He bows.

LAMA (*to baby puppet*)
Goodbye, old friend.

The baby puppet clings to the lama.

OLDEST BOY
Don't leave.

LAMA
I will come back soon.

OLDEST BOY
Please.

The puppet holds on to the lama's leg. The puppet cries.

LAMA
You can have this until I come back.

The lama gives his bell to the boy, and the boy rings the bell, delighted.

LAMA
Now you are happy. Good.
(*to the mother*) Thank you for your hospitality.

MOTHER
Of course.

LAMA
Goodbye!

MONK
Thank you, thank you. Goodbye!

They bow and leave. The father sees them out.

MOTHER
Oh my God.

OLDEST BOY
Why are you talking to God, Mama?

MOTHER
Oh, I wasn't talking to God, I was just—

OLDEST BOY
Mama, what is God?

MOTHER
God is here.

She touches her hand to his chest.

OLDEST BOY
No, that is my heart. Is God heart?
Bell! Heart! Mind! God!

He laughs.

MOTHER
What did you say?

OLDEST BOY
I said I want cornflakes. Mama, I have a question to tell you. Is there cornflakes? I'm starving.

MOTHER
Yes, I'll get you cornflakes. That is something I can do.

FOUR

The boy puppet sits at a table and eats cornflakes.
The mother calls her mother on the phone.

MOTHER
Hello, Mom?
So, I have something to tell you.
Mom, apparently—so, apparently, Tenzin might be a reincarnated
lama.
No, not like the animal. One *l*. Lama. It means teacher.

(*A long pause in which her mother says, "I don't understand. How do
they know?"*)

MOTHER
Well . . . apparently, an oracle saw a vision on a sacred lake—lake!
And the teacher told his student before he died
that he would take a Western reincarnation.

(*Pause.*)

MOTHER
No, not the Dalai Lama—that's a whole other thing—no, there
are a lot of reincarnated lamas, apparently.

Just, Mom—
Mom—the point is—they want to do a formal examination,
and if he passes—they might want to
take Tenzin to a monastery in India,
to educate him.

Mom. I need advice.
Not a divorce. *Advice.*
Look—
I'll call you later. I love you too.

She hangs up.
She puts her head in her hands.
The boy puppet walks over to her.

OLDEST BOY
What's wrong, Mama?

He touches her cheek gently with his hand.

MOTHER
Nothing, sweetheart.

OLDEST BOY
Don't be sad.
Can I watch *Sesame Street*?

MOTHER
Yes.

She puts on Sesame Street.
She puts him on her lap and watches with him.

MOTHER
I can't give you up.

OLDEST BOY
Shh, Mama, it's the big bird.

They watch.

OLDEST BOY
I love Big Bird.

FIVE

The official examination.
The monk starts laying out objects on the table.

LAMA

We will now place many objects on the table, three of which belonged to my teacher in his previous life. We will ask your son to choose the ones that belonged to him.

FATHER

La so.
(Yes.)

MOTHER

And if he gets any of them wrong—

LAMA

Then he is not my teacher.

The monks put an array of objects before the boy puppet—prayer
  beads, bowls, and prayer books.
The mother and father watch.

LAMA
So. Tenzin. Which one of these is yours?

A pause. The boy puppet considers.

OLDEST BOY
My beads. Mine.

LAMA
Yes.
And which of these?
Do you recognize anything?

The boy considers a bowl.
He picks one with a cracked side.

LAMA
But that one is broken.
Wouldn't you prefer one that is not broken?

OLDEST BOY
No. Mine.

MOTHER
Is that the one?

The monk nods to her.

MOTHER
Oh!

LAMA
And? Anything else?

The puppet considers.

OLDEST BOY
My book of prayers.

LAMA
Yes!

The monk and the lama do a prostration to the boy.

MOTHER
I think I might break in half.

FATHER
I will be your glue.

OLDEST BOY
Look, Mama, I got beads, a book, and a bowl.

LAMA (*gently, to the mother*)
He passed his examination. He chose all the right objects.

FATHER
We are very honored that our family was chosen.

He looks at his wife.

FATHER
Yes?

She looks pained and nods.

LAMA (*to the mother*)
Could you imagine sending him to the monastery?

MOTHER
I'd rather not talk about it in front of—(*indicating the boy*).

LAMA
Of course.
Might we have a moment?

MOTHER
Tenzin, could you go play in your room for a moment?

OLDEST BOY
No, Mama.

FATHER
I will take him. Come Tenzin.

MONK
Shall I follow you?

FATHER
Please.

Father, monk, and oldest boy exit.
The lama and mother sit.

MOTHER

Rinpoche. I was thinking. If my son really is a—a reincarnated lama—perhaps *I* could learn what he needs to learn and educate him at home.

LAMA

Perhaps. It would be tricky. The tradition is an unbroken one, a living one; you might say it is still warm. The teachings never died out because they are transmitted from teacher to student, from person to person. You would have to meditate for eighteen years in a cave, maybe for many lifetimes, then transmit that experience of mind to your student.

MOTHER

I see. I think maybe I have some problems with the whole concept of reincarnation.

LAMA

Oh, I see.
Well. We believe that we are all reborn, but some people actually choose their own reincarnation. You might imagine a necklace with many beads. The beads are separate, individual lifetimes, but they are connected by one thread—consciousness. We believe that every creature in this world has at one point been your own mother. So even your worst enemy—at some point in time—this person was your mother.

MOTHER
So you were once my mother.

LAMA
Yes.

MOTHER
I didn't mean to say you were my worst enemy.

LAMA
I know.

MOTHER
I'm a little overwhelmed.

LAMA
Of course. I would never force you to give over your child. You are his mother. It would have to be done at the right time, voluntarily. Your son has had many lifetimes, he will know what he must do. Until then, please, don't be distressed, or worried.

He takes her hands.

MOTHER
I like to worry.

Tenzin reenters with the monk and his father.

OLDEST BOY (*to the lama*)
Rinpoche, I drew you a picture.

The lama takes it.

LAMA
A rainbow. Thank you, thank you. Very nice, Tenzin.
(*to the mother and father*): We will leave you now.
I brought a picture—of my former teacher—if you would like to
have.

The father takes the picture and touches it to his forehead, a gesture of
respect.
He gazes at the picture for a moment.
The oldest boy grabs it.

OLDEST BOY
Mine.

FATHER
Tenzin!
(*to the lama*): Thank you.

LAMA (*to the father, then the mother*)
Perhaps you could visit us in India sometime. See for yourself
what the monastery is like.

OLDEST BOY
Yes, I would very much like to see the monastery again.
(*bowing formally*)
Rinpoche.

They all bow.

The puppet bows and puts his hands in prayer position, as though he's
  been doing it his whole life.

The mother and father look at him.

SIX

Night.
The mother and father at home.
The child sleeps in his room.

MOTHER
I'm not giving him up.

FATHER
You would not be giving him up. We can move to India with
him—

MOTHER
To India?

FATHER
—so we can visit him on the weekends . . .

MOTHER
On the *weekends*! He's barely three! My God, the hospitals, the
water . . . I just gave up *breast-feeding*—

FATHER
Shh, you'll wake him.

MOTHER (*quieter*)

Why does every religion have stories about giving up your child? I always thought the Abraham story was so awful. Any God who would ask that . . .

FATHER

What is the Abraham story?

MOTHER

God comes down and says, "Abraham, kill your son to prove your faith in me." And so Abraham puts his son on a slab of rock and is about to stab him and God says, "What are you doing, Abraham, I was just kidding!"

FATHER

No one is asking us to kill our son.

MOTHER

But to give him away . . .

FATHER

Not to give him away. To educate him, from a young age. It's like training a child music prodigy—you have to train a reincarnated lama early, or with their special abilities they go crazy. I've seen it happen. It's very bad. You think I want to lose our son? You think I'm not sad?

MOTHER

I don't know—I can never tell with you.

FATHER
Of course I'm sad. I try not to show my sadness.

MOTHER
Can I see his picture?

He gives her the picture of the former Rinpoche. She looks at it.

MOTHER
I don't see the resemblance.

FATHER
It's not like that.

MOTHER
I know. But do you?

The father looks at the picture closely.

FATHER
You know, I think I met him once. He came to dinner at the restaurant. As he was leaving, he said, "I like your food, I think I'll come back." And he winked at me, which is, you know, very rare for a high lama. So I remembered.

MOTHER
He came back to eat your food.
That's funny.
You have to laugh.
Only I can't laugh.

FATHER

Our son was chosen not just for himself, but to benefit others. You must think bigger than being only a mother.

MOTHER

Only a mother? He came out of my body.

FATHER

Into the body of the world. That is the first separation. There are many separations to come. He will go to school. You will die. Even if he were not a monk, there would be many separations.

MOTHER

Children who are separated from their parents at a young age don't form secure attachments.

FATHER

I went to boarding school when I was five.

MOTHER

Exactly.

FATHER

I will not force you.

MOTHER

Obviously.

FATHER

You are his mother. You must be convinced by reason that this is the right thing.

MOTHER

Reason? He picked out a shiny bell—babies like shiny bells—

FATHER

You saw his certainty, his delight, his comfort with the monks, as though they were old friends?

MOTHER

Yes. And I don't care.

FATHER

When it was convenient, you wanted to be Buddhist. Now that it is inconvenient, you do not want to be Buddhist.

MOTHER

I would call this more than inconvenient.

FATHER

Well, yes.

MOTHER

Who would take care of him?

FATHER

Rinpoche would take care of him. His former student would become his teacher.

MOTHER

That's a beautiful idea when I'm thinking about someone else's child but it's not a beautiful idea when it's my child. It's horrific.

FATHER

You brought him into the world. Now he is the world's child. I'm sorry. I am sad to think of losing him too. But try not to be so small.

MOTHER

Sometimes I really hate you.

FATHER

What?

MOTHER

You can be so smug.

FATHER

Smug?

MOTHER

Self-satisfied in your correct view of the world.

FATHER

So you're saying I am correct?

MOTHER

Don't. I won't give him up. I'd run away with him first. I'd take him to—

FATHER

Where?

MOTHER

Ohio.

FATHER

You are threatening to run away with our child?

MOTHER	**FATHER**
Yes, I'll take him to my mother in Ohio.	I gave up my family for you!

The boy puppet comes out in his pajamas.

MOTHER

What are you doing up?

OLDEST BOY

I'm thirsty. I heard angry voices.

MOTHER

I'll get you some water.

OLDEST BOY

I had a dream of mountains. Very tall mountains.
On my own planet. Called Katmandu.
Where monkeys stole my flip-flops.

MOTHER

What?

The mother and father look at each other.

FATHER

Time to go back to sleep.
You can dream of monkeys.

OLDEST BOY

But I have a question.

FATHER

Yes.

OLDEST BOY

Can I have a glass of milk?
Also why is the sky visible but God is invisible?

FATHER

That's a good question.

OLDEST BOY

Also, how did God build himself out of himself?
Do prayers have magic in them?

Are prayers invisible?
Can you draw God, but little, so he fits on a piece of paper?
Why is the mailman not as big as God?
How big is God?

FATHER (*stretching out his hands*)
This big.

OLDEST BOY
No! No, Papa!
The number five is a big number, but not as big as God!
Zero is a big number and it *is* as big as God!
Ha ha ha! Ha ha ha!

MOTHER
Who taught you that?

OLDEST BOY
I made it up.

He yawns.

OLDEST BOY
I'm sleepy.

FATHER
I'll take him.

The father picks him up.

MOTHER (*indicating the couch*)
I'll sleep on the couch.

FATHER
As you wish.

The father exits with the boy.
The mother grabs a blanket.
She goes to the couch.
She is not sleepy.

She puts her head in her hands.
She kicks something.
She throws something. Or she might tear up the picture of the
  Rinpoche, then collect the pieces, horrified at what she's done.
She wails.
The boy pads out.

OLDEST BOY
Mama, I'm hot. I heard a noise.

MOTHER
Here, come sleep with me.

He snuggles up with her on the couch.

OLDEST BOY
Mama, would you like to be God?

MOTHER

No, I like being your mama.

OLDEST BOY

But if you were God, then dinosaurs couldn't eat you.

MOTHER

That's true. Now go to sleep.

The boy sleeps on his mother. She closes her eyes.

SEVEN

MOTHER
That night I had a dream.

A monk drew a circle on the floor, out of sand.
Tenzin was in the middle of the circle.
My husband was King Solomon. He was judging me.

The monk draws a large circle in the floor out of colored sand.
The boy puppet stands in the middle.

MOTHER
Then my husband said:

FATHER
Pull.

The lama enters.

MOTHER
The lama and I were pulling each of my boy's arms.
The lama appeared to exert no effort at all. He pulled, gently.
But I pulled so hard, I sweated and wept.

FATHER
Pull.

MOTHER
We began pulling again.
I pulled with all my strength.
Then the lama let go.

And I broke off my son's arm.

The puppet's arm comes off his body.
An extended moment.

MOTHER
The lama reattached his arm, as if by magic.
We looked to the king for judgment, but the king said nothing.
Then my son spoke:

OLDEST BOY
I'm sorry, Mama. I'm walking to my country now.

MOTHER
Write to me.

OLDEST BOY
I can't write.
Bye-bye.

MOTHER
Don't go!
Wait for me.

OLDEST BOY
I can't wait.

MOTHER
Go later!

OLDEST BOY
Later is now!
I love you, Mama.

The puppet walks away from her toward the lama.
If there are Tibetan dancers, they come onstage and do a dance.
The mother wakes up. The mother does not dance.

End of Act One.

Act Two

ONE

The mother sits in meditation again, as in Act One, facing the audience.
A year has passed. She is pregnant.
She is in India.
She is in a monastery, in an open courtyard.
Time appears to slow a little in Act Two; there is more time for silence and ritual.

The mother is better at meditating now.
She opens her eyes for a moment,
sees the audience, and goes back to meditating.
Her cell phone rings.
It startles her.

MOTHER
Hello? Hello? Oh!
Hi, Mom. Hi.
I'm sorry I've been a little bit out of touch.
We're in—um—India.

Sorry, sorry—I should have told you we were leaving the country. Don't panic.

My doctor said I could travel until I'm thirty-six weeks.

That's why I didn't want to tell you, I knew you'd panic. We'll go back to the States to have the baby. Yes, in a hospital. With a doctor. No midwife.

We're here—to see the monastery. To sort of—check it out. Tenzin wanted to. He kept asking. I thought—if he could see it again—I mean if he could see it—he would sort of forget about it. And then I'd have the baby, and we'd all go back to normal. Sort of.

But now that we're here, they'd like to enthrone him. No it's— we can still take him home after—he wouldn't enter the monastery until he was much older.

(*Her mother says: "How old?"*)

MOTHER

Um, five? I know, I know! Mom, did you get my message? I left you a message. I wanted to invite you to the enthronement. *The enthronement.*

Yes, you would need shots.

Yes, I know it's crazy, I just thought I would ask. Yes, I'll send you pictures. Lots of pictures.

(*Her mother says: "What would your father have said about all this?*
'In the summer I'm a nudist; in the winter I'm a Buddhist.'")

MOTHER

What? In the summer I'm a nudist; in the winter I'm a Buddhist . . . Yes, I remember, Dad used to say that.

I love you too. Bye.

She hangs up.
Tenzin enters dressed in Tibetan clothes.

OLDEST BOY (*presses his forehead to her forehead in a greeting*)
Mama!

MOTHER
Sweetheart!

OLDEST BOY
Udu.

MOTHER (*pressing her forehead to his forehead*)
Udu.

She points to his feet, teaching him the Tibetan word for feet.

MOTHER
Kang pa.
(Feet.)

OLDEST BOY
Kang pa.

MOTHER (*pointing to his hands*)
Lak pa.
(Hands.)

OLDEST BOY
Lak pa.

MOTHER (*touching his ears*)
Am-chog.
(Ears.)

OLDEST BOY
Am-chog.
That tickles.
Rinpoche says today I get a haircut.

MOTHER
Oh? Today?

OLDEST BOY
Yes. Only I like my hair.

MOTHER
I like your hair too.

OLDEST BOY
Then don't let them cut it.

MOTHER
Don't worry. It'll feel soft on your head. Like a duckling. You like ducklings?

OLDEST BOY
I don't like ducklings. I love ducklings.
Mama, will you miss me when I am on the throne?

MOTHER (*holding back tears*)
Yes.

OLDEST BOY
What's in your eyes, Mama?
Why do you have eyelashes?
I love your eyes, Mama.

MOTHER
Thank you.

OLDEST BOY
Why do I have brown eyes and you don't, Mama?

MOTHER
Because your daddy has brown eyes.

OLDEST BOY
And your daddy doesn't have brown eyes?

MOTHER
No.

OLDEST BOY
Where is your daddy?

MOTHER
He's in heaven.

OLDEST BOY
Oh yes. I remember. Why is he in heaven?

MOTHER
He died.

OLDEST BOY
Why did he die?

MOTHER
He got old. And sick.
His body broke.

OLDEST BOY
I will never let you get old, Mama.
I will never let you die.

MOTHER
Thank you.

The monk and the father walk in together.
The mother bows to the monk.

MONK (*to the boy*)
Hello!
Today we cut your hair!

OLDEST BOY
No!

FATHER
Tenzin.

MONK
Don't worry. I will be very gentle.

MOTHER
Do we have to do it today?

FATHER
It's better to get it over with.

MONK (*to the mother*)
Is it okay?

The mother nods.
The monk soaps the boy's hair with water from a bucket.
At first the boy is calm, then suddenly:

OLDEST BOY
Papa! Don't let them cut my hair!

FATHER
It's okay. I'll hold your hand.

The boy puppet cries.
The monk tries to cut his hair.

OLDEST BOY
No!

MONK (*to the mother and father*)
Maybe it's better if you're not here for this?

FATHER
Yes, I think so. Be a good boy, Tenzin.

The mother and father retreat, out of view of the boy.

OLDEST BOY
Mama! Papa!

MONK
It's okay, Tenzin. You will see how nice it feels to have a nice close haircut.

The monk starts to shave the boy puppet's head with a razor so that he has the closely cropped hair of a monk.

OLDEST BOY
No haircut!

The boy won't keep still.

MONK
You are a good boy. Can you stay still? Do you want to fly your plane while I cut your hair?

OLDEST BOY
Yes.

The boy flies his remote plane while his hair is cut.
The plane is really a puppet.
The boy calms down.
The monk shaves the boy's head.

MONK
Okay, okay. Good job.

Hair falls to the floor.
The mother and father hide, watching from a distance.
The father wipes away a tear.

MONK
Look at that airplane! Like magic, right? Who is flying that plane? Are you flying that plane?

OLDEST BOY
Yes.

MONK
Where is the airplane going?

OLDEST BOY
Katmandu. Where my flip-flops got stolen by monkeys.

MONK
Your flip-flops were stolen by monkeys?

OLDEST BOY

Yes. At a temple.

MONK

Oh! That is true! I remember that! Oh, we must tell Rinpoche that you remember when in your previous life your flip-flops got stolen by monkeys!

The mother and father look at each other.
It is rare even for reincarnated lamas to remember their previous lives.

OLDEST BOY

Is my head smooth now?

MONK

Yes! Now let's go tell Rinpoche all about the monkeys.

OLDEST BOY (*while leaving*)
Naughty monkeys.

MONK

Yes. Naughty, naughty monkeys.

The monk walks offstage with the boy, who goes willingly.
The mother and father watch them go.
The mother begins collecting her boy's hair, scooping it with her hands.
It is hard for her to bend down with her big belly.

FATHER
Don't bend down. I'll get his hair.

He finishes collecting the hair.

MOTHER
I want to keep it.
Can he really remember Katmandu?

FATHER
It's possible.

MOTHER
I want to go home.

FATHER
Yes, I know what you mean.

MOTHER
You do? I'm not even sure what I mean. Sometimes I'll be home and I'll think, I want to go home—but I'm already home. Do you ever do that? Do you ever sit right in our living room and think, I want to go home?

FATHER
Yes.

MOTHER
Of course, you're in exile, that was stupid. I'm sorry.

FATHER

It's okay.

He breathes in.

FATHER

This is what my nights smelled like when I was a boy.

MOTHER

Do you think of yourself as being from India at all? Or only Tibet?

FATHER

Sometimes I feel that my mother was my country. And she died. So now I have no country.

The mother nods.

MOTHER

You don't talk about your mother.

FATHER

No?

MOTHER

No.

FATHER

It's not good to talk about dead people too much. If you do, they'll stay attached to this world, they won't get a good rebirth.

MOTHER
I didn't know that. I thought you would cry and I would comfort you. I thought I was a bad wife—because you wouldn't share your sadness with me.

FATHER
That's silly.

MOTHER
I guess it is. I thought you were mad.

FATHER
Not mad, sad.

He takes her hand.

MOTHER
Oh.
Do you remember your childhood home, in Tibet?

FATHER
I remember low ceilings, dark wood, an altar room. We left quickly, at night. There wasn't much time to say goodbye.

MOTHER
Who lives in it now?

FATHER
My uncle says it's being used as a classroom.

MOTHER
Oh, that's good—

FATHER
To teach Chinese language to Tibetan children.

MOTHER
Oh my God.

FATHER
Shhh. Rest. You must be tired.

MOTHER
I can't sleep. I want to tuck Tenzin in.

FATHER
I know.

MOTHER
What should we do with his hair?

Night starts to come on with all of its night noises.
The mother rests on the father for a moment.
On the other side of the stage,
the monk prepares a bed for the boy.
He tucks the boy puppet in.

MONK
Good night.

The monk lies on the floor and sleeps near the boy.
The moon appears in the sky.
The boy looks at it.
The parents look at it.
Boy and parents look at the same moon, missing each other.
The mother rubs her belly.

MOTHER
She's kicking.

FATHER
She?

MOTHER
It's a girl. It has to be. If she's a girl, she can't be a lama.
I can't stop thinking about Mary.

FATHER
Mary?

MOTHER
You know, Mary? And Joseph? When Jesus ran away to teach,
he was twelve. That night, when his parents couldn't find him,
did they pray for him to be ordinary? "Please, please let my son
be ordinary." Did they want to keep his kindness for themselves?
Were they proud? Angry? Or only worried? Once you have children, does worry become a placeholder for thought?

The father nods.

FATHER
I wonder if he's sleeping.

MOTHER
Our boy?

FATHER (*with emotion*)
Our boy.

Pause.

MOTHER
Are we leaving Tenzin here or taking him back home?

FATHER
I don't know.
What do you want to do?

MOTHER
That's the first time you've asked me.

FATHER
So I'm asking: What do you want to do? You're his mother. I will leave it up to you.

MOTHER
I have this strange feeling that it's no longer a choice, that he's no longer mine.

Pause.

FATHER (*with emotion*)

Now that you've given way, it is me who doesn't want to let him go.

The lights change to morning light.
The father exits, to go put on his ceremonial robes for the
  enthronement.

TWO

The lama enters, praying.

MOTHER
Good morning, Rinpoche.

LAMA
Ah, good morning.

He takes her hands.

LAMA
How are you feeling today?

MOTHER
Fine. I'm surviving the heat.

LAMA
Good, good.
That's not what I meant.

MOTHER
I know.

LAMA

So. After your husband gets his robes on, I will teach you both where to stand. You will both stand in line and be blessed by your son too.

MOTHER

Okay.

LAMA

Okay.

MOTHER

Rinpoche. May I ask you something?

LAMA

Of course.

MOTHER

Do you remember being taken away from your mother to go to the monastery?

LAMA

Yes.

MOTHER

Was it hard for you?

LAMA

Yes, it was hard. I cried. I missed her. I was the son of simple farming people. Then suddenly I was surrounded by fancy people,

people bowing to me. I missed my mother and my siblings. Then, I remember one time, I was missing my mother very much, and then I thought of my teacher, who was my mother and my father both. I thought, I have two mothers and two fathers, so why am I crying? And after that I was fine.

MOTHER
I see.

LAMA
I must thank you. I remember when my teacher died, I cried for three days. When he was alive, there was order in the universe. He always cared for me, he showed me what to do, and when he died, I didn't know what to do, how to carry on with my task. But then I met your son, and there is purpose again.

MOTHER
Yes. It was the same for me when my teacher died.

LAMA
Your teacher died?

MOTHER
Yes.

LAMA
And what did you do when your teacher died, to find purpose again?

MOTHER

I got pregnant.

He laughs.

LAMA

No, really.

MOTHER

Really.

LAMA

But you must keep up your investigation for your teacher, no?

MOTHER

After he died it seemed pointless. Books about books. I wanted to be a better person.

LAMA

Perhaps you could write a book that would make people better?

She laughs.

MOTHER

I'm afraid you're overestimating Western academia. Anything with a practical application, or to do with virtue, is forbidden. At my university it felt like adults were squabbling like children much of the time.

LAMA
You have never seen monks debate.

MOTHER
No.

LAMA
I will take you sometime.

MOTHER
I would like that.

LAMA
So in your university, what did they squabble about?

MOTHER
Oh, well. There's this thing called deconstructionism? It's very boring. But I believe it killed my teacher.

LAMA
An idea killed your teacher?

MOTHER
Kind of.

LAMA
How?

MOTHER
At my oral exam—

LAMA

Oral exam—

MOTHER

Where your teachers ask you questions but really argue with each other and show off—

LAMA

Yes, yes—we have—

MOTHER

So this one professor, my second reader—a terrifying woman—said to me, "I really don't understand how you left Heidegger off your reading list. It's a major oversight." I opened my mouth, but no words came out. My adviser saw my distress, and he said, "She ignored Heidegger because Heidegger was a Nazi." The woman professor said, "Well, that's reductive, isn't it?" And my teacher said, "So was the Holocaust." She said, "I'm not sure I follow." My teacher said, "The Holocaust reduced my people by six million Jews." She said, "I don't think that's fair to bring up in the context of an intellectual argument about being." My teacher said, "And I do. Some Jews lived. Most didn't. How's that for being and nonbeing." Then his face turned white, and he said, "It's convenient to say history was a construct when you've been on the wrong side of it." Then his head fell down on his desk, he had a massive stroke, and he died. And I always blamed myself.

LAMA

But your teacher's death was not your fault.

MOTHER

Maybe. If only I'd read Heidegger, if only I . . . I don't know.

LAMA

Every person has his time to die. We have only so many breaths in the body. It was your teacher's time.

MOTHER

I suppose.

LAMA

After your teacher died, did you get another teacher?

MOTHER

No. There was a search committee. They found a young Marxist who thought the word "spiritual" had no meaning.

LAMA

No, communists do not like religion.

MOTHER

No.

LAMA

But your teacher—

MOTHER

My teacher was interested in the relationship between virtue and books, so he was very unfashionable at the university. He was this wonderful dinosaur, with an office full of dusty books; he'd read more than anyone. He said to me once, "You don't want me as your thesis adviser. I'm unfashionable." "I don't care," I said. And then he asked, "You want to know how never to become unfashionable? Never become fashionable. Stay home and read." And so I did.

LAMA

Would you like me to make an offering for your teacher, to pray that he has a good rebirth?

MOTHER

My teacher was Jewish. He didn't believe in reincarnation.

LAMA

What did he believe in?

MOTHER

Literature. When I talked to him, my mind, and his mind, were very close.

LAMA

Yes.

She remembers her teacher.

MOTHER

I miss him.

The lama nods.

MOTHER
When I got pregnant, part of me thought, Maybe it's my teacher, coming back to see me.

LAMA
Ah! You *did* believe in reincarnation all along!

MOTHER
Maybe a little.

LAMA
I am sorry you lost your teacher.

MOTHER
Thank you.
I don't know that anyone ever said that to me. There is no—in our culture—sort of—ritual for losing your teacher. You just—lose them.

LAMA
It is very sad to lose your teacher.

She nods.
She sees that he is her new teacher.
She takes a deep breath.

MOTHER
Do you think . . .

LAMA (*he reads her mind*)
Yes, you are a good mother.

MOTHER
How did you do that?
Are you in the business of reading minds?

He laughs.
A moment.

MOTHER
Sometimes I think good mothers have to think they're bad, just in case, and it's only bad mothers who think they're good. Like: to keep a plane in the sky you have to constantly worry that it will fall down.

He laughs.

LAMA
No, no. My teacher chose you. You must be good.

MOTHER
Thank you.
I've been meaning for a long time—ever since I married my husband—to take refuge. But I haven't done it. I was afraid. I was waiting to meet the right teacher.

He nods.

MOTHER
Might I take refuge with you?

LAMA
Of course.

MOTHER
I'd like to do it before Tenzin is enthroned.

LAMA
Okay. We have a little time.

MOTHER
Now?

LAMA
If you wish.

MOTHER
Don't you need any—stuff—or other people or—bells—or books?

LAMA
No no, just a teacher—and a student. Simple. Okay?

MOTHER
Okay.
Here we go.

LAMA
Is it okay for you to kneel?

MOTHER
Yes.

She kneels.

LAMA
Do you know the vows?

MOTHER
I think so.

LAMA
Repeat after me.

Horns. Bells. One ceremony leads into another.

Ceremony Three

Music.
The mother and father dress in traditional Tibetan clothes for a
*   ceremony.*
The boy puppet is dressed in monastic robes.
A ceremonial hat is placed on the boy's head.
The puppeteer is also now dressed as a monk.

A procession.
Chanting.
If you have a chorus of Tibetan dancers,
they might create a procession or a dance.

The lama puts the boy puppet on a throne.
The boy receives and gives a white scarf—or khata—*and a blessing*
*   to everyone who passes by him.*
The mother and father go up to be blessed by him.
They bow their heads in front of him.
The boy blesses his father.
The boy blesses his mother.
The mother tries not to cry.
The chorus of women weeps with the mother
but restrain their tears.
The mother and father move away.

Many people go to be blessed by the boy.
He pats each of their heads naturally.

Finally, the lama goes to be blessed by his former teacher.

The puppet suddenly disappears
and is replaced by the puppeteer.

The puppeteer, now a grown-up lama, touches his forehead to his
former student's head.

OLDEST BOY
Hello again, my friend.

LAMA
Rinpoche.

His former student weeps in recognition.
An extended moment while the teacher blesses the student.
The mother looks up at her boy, but he is an old man now.
She is confused.

Loud chanting.
Horns and drums.

The mother looks for her boy.
Her husband tugs on her sleeve to get her to sit down.

MOTHER
Where is he?

FATHER
He's there, right there.

MOTHER
I can't see him.

FATHER
He's there.

MOTHER
I don't feel good.

FATHER
It's hot.

MOTHER
No, I don't feel good.
I need to go. No, I need *to go.*
NOW.

THREE

The chanting gives way to
a scene of giving birth.

MOTHER
No. It's too early it's too early . . .
No no no—
I want to go home I want to have this baby at home . . . airplane!
I need an airplane . . .

The monk enters.

MONK
Is everything okay?
I was worried when I saw you leaving the prayer hall so suddenly.

FATHER
I think she's having a baby.

MOTHER
No, it's too early, too early . . .

FATHER
Stay calm . . . it's all right . . .

MOTHER

It's a month early!

Hospital, where is the hospital?

MONK

This is your hospital for now. We will take care of you.

MOTHER

Oh God! My mother would kill me.

The father soothes her.

MOTHER

Oh, it hurts.

Do you have epidurals in India?

Epidural please! I'll have an epidural please!

MONK

Yes, we have, but not in the guesthouse of a monastery!

MOTHER

Who is going to deliver this baby?

MONK

Sometimes, in Tibet, the women they deliver their own babies.

MOTHER

Nooooooooo!

FATHER
It's okay. I will do it.

MOTHER
Oh my God!

MONK
You will be fine.
Don't be alarmed. It must be quite simple.

MOTHER
Oh! I want an epidural! I want my mother!

The monk prays with his prayer beads.

FATHER (*in Tibetan*)
Chu tsa bo kang kher sho. Cham ze khersho.
(Can you get me hot water and a scissors?)

MONK (*in Tibetan*)
La so!
(Yes!)

MOTHER
What?

The monk runs out.

FATHER
Breathe. Breathe.

MOTHER
Aaaaa! I'm not ready. I'm not ready.

FATHER
Push!

MOTHER
Aaaaa!

She pushes.

FATHER
Good!

MOTHER
It hurts!

FATHER
I know! I'm sorry.
Push!

She labors.

MOTHER
Where's Tenzin? Is he all right? I don't remember where Tenzin is?

FATHER
Rinpoche is watching him.

MOTHER
Oh, oh good.

FATHER
Push.

She pushes.

FATHER
Good! Good! I think that's the head!

MOTHER
OOOOOOOOH!
I want my boy.

Tenzin walks in, now an old man, not a puppet.

OLDEST BOY
I am here, Mama.

MOTHER
Oh, good.
I missed you. Hold my hand.

OLDEST BOY
Okay, Mama.

He strokes her hair.
The baby comes out.

The baby cries.
The mother cries.

MOTHER
Oh, God! What is it what is it?

FATHER
A girl!

MOTHER
Oh, thank God!
Is she okay?

FATHER
She's beautiful. Perfect nose. Perfect hands. All the parts. Oh, she's slippery.
Let me just—hold still—let me cut the cord.

The monk hands the father little sterile scissors.
The father cuts the cord.
The sound of a bell.
The father wraps the baby in a
blanket and hands her to the mother.

MOTHER
Hello. Hello.
You, you—will not be a monk.
No one will take you away from me.

THE OLDEST BOY
Can I hold her?

MOTHER
Be gentle. Hold her head up.

THE OLDEST BOY
I know, Mama. I've done this before. I used to be your father, remember?

MOTHER
What?

THE OLDEST BOY
Many lifetimes ago. I held you in my arms, like this.

The mother hands Tenzin the bundle of blankets that is the baby.
He holds the baby.
A bell.

Epilogue

The mother slowly stands and speaks to the audience.

MOTHER

We stayed in India for two months. In India, after you give birth, you're treated like a queen. For forty days you don't go outside. People feed you. We visited Tenzin at the monastery every week. He seemed content there. One day he told me to go home. "Home, where?" I asked. "America," he said. "My home is here now. You go to your home."

So my husband and I, and our girl, we went home. We reopened the restaurant. I reopened my books. I became addicted to translation. From Tibetan into English and back again. I started to think that translation was a little like reincarnation. You jump from one language into another, and there is something in between . . .

I worry that someday my son will hate me for having given him away. That reincarnation was just a pretty idea. And the cruel animal fact of motherhood is bigger than any idea. But every night, before I go to sleep, my son quietly enters my room. He whispers, "Can I sleep here, Mama?"

The boy puppet enters and stands beside the mother, holding her hand.

And I think—how could it be? Did he run from the monastery? How can he be there and also here, next to me? There he was, sleeping peacefully in my bed, a child at night, and there he was in the monastery, a grown man in the light of day, with many lifetimes behind him, relearning what he already knew before. In the morning when I wake up, he's not there.

And that's the end of this play. Or the beginning. They are sometimes hard to tell apart. And it's difficult to go from one to the other. To say good morning is easy. To say good night is hard. Good night (*to the puppet*).

OLDEST BOY
Good night, Mama.

The puppet starts to walk offstage.
He waves to his mother.
She waves back.
The puppet cuts his own strings.
The mother runs after him.
The puppet falls to the ground.
The puppeteer stands, arms outstretched.

OLDEST BOY
Don't worry. I'm here.

The mother goes to him.
The puppeteer becomes the boy and hugs his mother.

The end.
The beginning.
The end.
The beginning.
The end.

Playwright's Afterword in the Form of Five Questions

1. How did a Catholic girl from Illinois come to write about Tibetan Buddhism?

I have three children. For eight years we've had a wonderful babysitter named Yangzom. She is from Queens, by way of India, by way of Tibet. Because I often work from home, often writing in the dining room, Yangzom and I have gotten to know each other very well. We have shared the strange intimacy of sitting in a room together as she gave a bottle to one of my newborn twins while I breast-fed the other baby. We have administered nebulizers and Tylenol to sick children together, celebrated birthdays together, and rejoiced in first steps together.

Over the years, she has told me many stories about life in exile in India and what it was like to escape Tibet with the Chinese army in pursuit, her twelve-day-old daughter strapped on her back as she navigated the Himalayas. When her mother came from Nepal for her first visit to the United States, they visited our home. Yangzom knelt at her mother's feet, as was the custom, and her mother smiled at my children and silently prayed for hours. I was raised in a small town in Illinois—and the world was getting both bigger and smaller. When Yangzom lived in India, she sent her children to boarding school in Darjeeling, the same English boarding school, oddly, that my Thai father-in-law attended. The world continued to get smaller, and I, an ambivalent

Catholic from Illinois, learned more and more about Tibetan Buddhism and the beauty and resilience of Tibetan culture. This play is dedicated to Yangzom because a story she told me brought this play about.

Three years ago she told me about Tibetan friends of hers in Boston who had a successful restaurant. One day, monks from India arrived to tell the family that their son was a reincarnated lama, or high teacher. I said, "Well, what did they do???" Yangzom said, "They closed the restaurant and moved to India to educate the child at a monastery." Having three kids myself, it seemed incomprehensible to let go of a child with any grace, even if it was for their own spiritual development. I wanted to write about the subject, but I felt that if there was to be dramatic conflict, there had better be a woman not culturally raised to be a Buddhist in the play. I was interested in exploring the dynamic between the "attachment parenting" phenomenon in certain mothering circles in the United States and a vague interest that the same set of people might have in Buddhism, which emphasizes nonattachment.

Every day, as I wave to my children when I drop them off at school or let one of them have a new experience—like crossing the street without holding my hand—I experience the struggle between love and nonattachment. It is hard to bear—the extreme love of one's child and the thought that ultimately the child belongs to the world. There is this horrible design flaw—children are supposed to grow up and away from you, and one of you will die first.

Motherhood is a predicament. How to live fully inside of it with any grace? And how to write about it?

2. Why a puppet?

When considering writing a play about a child who was a reincarnated spiritual master, I wondered how I would cast that role with a three-year-old who could memorize lines, project, and evince the spiritual authority of a seventy-year-old lama. This seemed an almost impossible task. Since three-year-olds aren't very reliable, I decided to use a puppet. I've always wanted to work with puppets, and I felt that the puppet would be the clearest way to see the child and the child's previous life at the same time. I wanted there to be little or no doubt in the play that the child was in fact a reincarnation, so that the characters in the play, when presented with the news, could be more concerned with the question of "Now what?" rather than, to my mind, the less interesting question of "Is he or isn't he?"

The metaphor of the puppet and the puppeteer is meant to connect the child, or body, with the older spirit that animates the child. I was not interested in the cliché of the puppet as an object to be manipulated. Eric Bass, a puppet maker, says it better than I can in his wonderful essay "The Myths of Puppet Theater":

> There are two myths about puppet theater that need to be exploded. The first of them . . . is the myth that the puppeteer controls the puppet. This myth is, of course, supported by numerous catch phrases in our language and culture: *He played him like a puppet. Puppet government.* All suggest that the puppeteer makes the puppet do whatever he or she wants. Although some puppeteers do try to impose their will on the objects of their art, most know that this is a disservice to both the art and the object. Our job, our *art*, is to bring the puppet to life. To

impose control over the object is, in both spirit and practice, the opposite of this.

As puppeteers, it is, surprisingly, *not* our job to impose our intent on the puppet. It is our job to discover what the puppet can do and what it seems to want to do. It has propensities. We want to find out what they are, and support them. We are, in this sense, less like tyrants, and more like nurses to these objects . . . They seem to have destinies. We want to help them arrive at those destinies . . . It requires from us a generosity. If we try to dominate them, we will take from them the life we are trying to give them.

3. *Have there ever been Western reincarnations of Tibetan lamas?*

Although this play is utterly a fiction, there are a handful of Tibetan lamas who have been reincarnated in the West, sometimes to white parents, or to intercultural parents. I had the good fortune to meet with one such *tulku* when he was all grown up. His mother was American and his father was French, and both were Tibetan Buddhists. He was recognized as a reincarnate lama at the age of three and enthroned in a monastery in India. I asked him how his mother was able to make such a decision. He said that she was very clear in her decision because he himself as a three-year-old expressed a strong desire to go to the monastery. Much of her pain came from the cultural opprobrium of other French mothers, who didn't understand her decision.

As it becomes more and more difficult to openly practice Buddhism in Tibet because of the Chinese occupation, it becomes more common for high teachers to choose reincarnations outside of Tibet. Tibetan Buddhists believe that while all of us are reborn, high spiritual masters are reincarnated, meaning they get to choose their new life, and often they choose a context that will be most fruitful to them in continuing their life's work.

I was first introduced to the concept of the *tulku* system, by which the student searches for the reincarnation of his former teacher, in the beautiful documentary *Unmistaken Child*. I was so moved by the idea that a student could find a teacher again, and that the student becomes the teacher, and the teacher becomes the student, lifetime after lifetime. I have been very lucky in my own life to have extraordinary teachers. I was comforted by the idea that I might have known them before and might know them again.

4. How is my life different from a Tibetan's living in Tibet?

I am free to learn and study in my own language. I can leave my country and return. I have a passport. I am a citizen of my country. I can pray without going to jail. I am not asked to denounce my god or to walk on pictures of what I consider sacred. My house and my church have not been summarily destroyed by an occupying nation. I can own a picture of my spiritual or secular leader without going to jail. I can write a book about my life, or tell stories of the past to my children, and not go to jail.

If I went to jail, I would get a lawyer. I would not be held indefinitely for decades by Chinese officials. I would not have my arms and feet shackled as I was suspended from the ceiling. I would not watch as nuns were raped even though they had taken vows of chastity. I would not be doused with boiling water. I would not be urinated on by guards. I would not have bamboo shoots placed under my fingernails. I would be visited. I would be fed.

5. Given that my life is so very different from life in Tibet, what right have I to write Tibetan characters?

I ask myself that question every day we rehearse this play. I remind myself of what I have in common with an average mother or father living in Tibet: I love my children. I want the best for them. It hurts me when they are sick or when I'm parted from them. I wonder what it's like to die. I love my teachers. I miss my father. I wonder how it is that we are all connected despite our tremendous differences.

There is a saying: the five world religions are like the five fingers of the hand, pointing to the same moon. And I wonder, along with my children: What is the moon?

Acknowledgments

I was moved and inspired by the beautiful documentary *Unmistaken Child*. I am extremely grateful for conversations with Lama Pema, for his gentleness and wisdom, and for his visits to the cast. I am also grateful for conversations with Lama Karma Drodhul, Chusang Rinpoche, Geshe Lobsang Dhargye, Lama Kathy Wesley, the amazing Annabella Pitkin, Trinlay Rinpoche, and Giselle de Saint Phalle, Tsondu Kikhangparra, Jampal Namgel, Namgel Norbu, Mark Epstein, Virginia Blum, Dominique Townsend, and Tim McHenry of the Rubin Museum. We could not have done *The Oldest Boy* without the invaluable presence and generous expertise of Tsering Dorjee Bawa. Our partnership with the Tibet Fund, specifically with Rinchen Dharlo and Lobsang Nyandak, was indispensable, and I am so grateful to both men for their time and energy and help. I am incredibly grateful to Thupten Jinpa and Gelek Rimpoche for all their teaching and scholarship and for visiting us at Lincoln Center.

Some incredibly helpful books were *The Tibetan Book of Living and Dying* by Sogyal Rinpoche, *Comes the Peace* by Daja Wangchuk Meston, *Across Many Mountains* by Yangzom Brauen, *Reborn in the West: The Reincaranation Masters* by Vicki Mackenzie, *Dragon Thunder* by Diana Mukpo, *The Monk and the Philosopher* by Jean-François Revel and Matthieu Ricard, and *The Way of the White Clouds* by Lama Anagarika Govinda. I am grateful to have read the beautiful autobiographies of the Dalai Lama, *My Land and My People*; of the Dalai Lama's mother, *Dalai Lama, My Son: A Mother's Story*; and of his brother, *Tibet Is My Country*, by Thubten Jigme Norbu. Also the books of Lama Yeshe and Stephen Batchelor. And *The Deconstruction of Literature: Criticism After Auschwitz* by my beloved professor David Hirsch. I also recommend the documentaries *Yangsi: Reincarnation Is Just the Beginning*; *Compassion in Exile: The Life of the 14th Dalai Lama*; and *My Reincarnation*. Finally, I love the books of Jetsunma Tenzin Palmo and am grateful to have taken refuge with her.

I also want to thank my earliest readers: Bruce Ostler and Tony. And to the group who did the first reading at the Piven Theatre Workshop: Polly Noonan, Joe Foronda, Richard Manera, Joel Kim Booster, Rinzing Dorge, Sharup Gyatso, and Adam Belcuore and Rinzing, who assembled the cast. Jessica Thebus was also present and has taught me about art, motherhood, and generosity over a decades-long conversation.

The biggest debt of gratitude goes to Yangzom, who brings so much care into our lives every day. She offered me the beginnings of this story and so much help along the way. Thank you to Tony, Anna, William, and Hope. Thank you to Kate Ruhl and Kathy Ruhl, and to the Noonans of Tryon Farm, and Clubbed Thumb and Two Rivers for space and time to write. And I want to thank the team of designers I worked with—Matt, Anita, Mimi, Darron, Barney, and Japhy—I couldn't have asked for a more beautiful collaboration. And thank you to Anne Cattaneo for her intelligent and game spirit and generosity. To André Bishop for his strength and wisdom and for opening his home to me again and again. And to the cast—James, Jimmy, Tsering, Ernest, Takemi, Nami, Jon, and incandescent Celia—there is not a more compassionate, steadfast cast, nor one that is as much fun to be in a room with. And to the actors we workshopped the play with who also shared their gifts—Joel, Daniel, and Francis. Thank you to the tireless and unflappable Daniel Swee for assembling said actors. Finally, to Rebecca Taichman—who has such a strong heart, loves writers so passionately, comes to the theater every day to ask big questions about death, love, and how we should treat each other in this lifetime. She created a little utopia every day we rehearsed together.

This play is about the bond between mother and child as well as about the bond between teacher and students. And so I would like to thank my mother. And all my students who have taught me while I was writing this play; in particular, Max Ritvo, the oldest young soul I know—you have taught me so much. And to the playwrights Amelia Roper and MJ Kaufman, whose use of puppets in her beautiful *Sagittarius Ponderosa* made me think about puppets in a new way. And thank you to my teachers, from kindergarten up: Mrs. MacGregor, Mrs. Tachau, Mrs. Boland, Mr. Spangenberger, Mr. Kemp, Mr. Artebesi, Jane Schwalbach, Blossom Marmel, Eloise Fink, Larry Rehage, Raissa Landor, Caroline Erbman, William Duprey, David Konstan, Joseph Pucci, Beverly Baker, Jack Mattox, Coppelia Kahn, Mac Wellman, Maria Irene Fornes, Nilo Cruz, Ken Prestininzi, Jessica Thebus, Barbara Rubenstein, Professor Hirsch, Joyce Piven, and always Paula Vogel.